In an age where m
seeking to redefine
a 'fresh word from
to read a biblically

Most importantly, Neto's book gives us a God-entranced vision of missions. Built upon that foundation, the mission of God is explained from the Old to the New Testament to show God's love for the nations, as mediated by His covenant people, Israel. Discussions of cultural sensitivity, contextualization, postmodernism, globalization, technology, and living eschatologically are sure to make this volume a helpful conversation piece for the church.

Jonathan Moorhead
The Master's Academy International,
serving in Russia and the Czech Republic since 2008
(specializes in Church History, Theology, and
Apologetics)

It impressed me how Emilio masterfully treated this subject in less than one hundred pages. When he refers to 'mission' he is writing about the redemptive Work of God through all His servants (the workers) across the street and around the world. It is worth reading.

Elias Medeiros
Intercultural Studies, Professor of Missions
Emeritus, Reformed Theological Seminary

From the beginning of the world, God has worked to save a people for Himself, and nothing can give a young person more purpose and fulfillment than to see themselves as part of this global work—whether across the world or in their backyard. Emilio speaks skillfully to a younger generation about the joys, challenges, and responsibilities of mission work. His book is simple, straightforward, and relational in the way it communicates vibrant truth.

Simona Gorton
9Marks International Project Manager
Author of *Better Than We Dreamed*

This little book shows that mission is at the heart of God's purposes for the world, and challenges us to play our part in this urgent work.

Bill James
Principal, London Seminary, London

TRACK
DOCTRINE

EMILIO
GAROFALO NETO
SERIES EDITED BY
JOHN PERRITT

A STUDENT'S GUIDE TO
MISSIONS

CHRISTIAN
FOCUS

rym

Scripture quotations are from *The Holy Bible, English Standard Version*, copyright © 2001 by Crossway Bibles, a publishing ministry of Good News Publishers. Used by permission. All rights reserved. ESV Text Edition: 2011.

paperback ISBN 978-1-5271-0896-7
ebook ISBN 978-1-5271-0920-9

10 9 8 7 6 5 4 3 2 1

First published in 2022
by
Christian Focus Publications Ltd,
Geanies House, Fearn, Ross-shire,
IV20 1TW, Great Britain
www.christianfocus.com

with

Reformed Youth Ministries,
1445 Rio Road East
Suite 201D
Charlottesville,
Virginia, 22911

Cover by MOOSE77

Printed by Bell & Bain, Glasgow

CONTENTS

Series Introduction

Christianity is a religion of words, because our God is a God of words. He created through words, calls Himself the Living Word, and wrote a book (filled with words) to communicate to His children. In light of this, pastors and parents should take great efforts to train the next generation to be readers. *Track* is a series designed to do exactly that.

Written for students, the *Track* series addresses a host of topics in three primary areas: Doctrine, Culture, and the Christian Life. *Track's* booklets are theologically rich, yet accessible. They seek to engage and challenge the student without dumbing things down.

One definition of a track reads: *a way that has been formed by someone else's footsteps.* The goal of the *Track* series is to point us to that 'someone else'—Jesus Christ. The One who forged a track to guide His followers. While we cannot follow this track perfectly, by His grace and Spirit He calls us to strive to stay on the path. It is our prayer that this series of books would help guide Christ's Church until He returns.

In His service,

John Perritt
RYM's Director of Resources
Series Editor

Introduction

When John Perritt asked me to write about missions for this fine book series, I was both honored and intrigued. Honored, because writing about one of the foremost topics of Scripture is a matter of great joy, and I was happy to see how much confidence Perritt has in me for such a task. I was also intrigued. How to write about missions in a way that is biblical, winsome, useful, and not overly long? I pray that this book will instruct, encourage, and challenge you. My goal is very simple: to help you consider how missions are a necessary part of the Christian life. Not only that, but an honor that God confers on us.

1. Why Should I Care About Missions?

There is so much to think about every day. Our minds are filled to the brink with information, and life is buzzing with news, ideas, events and problems. There is so much always going on everywhere. But there is also so much going on in your little world. Just think of all you have to do today. Or, think of what you did yesterday.

Life is impressively busy. There is so much to see, so many chores to get to, so much work, so much study, so much entertainment available. Why should I even bother thinking about missions? Aren't they happening in remote lands, most of which I don't even know the name of? Don't we send missionaries to take care of this in our places? Shouldn't I be focusing on the here and now, especially considering how much I have on my plate? And especially at my age! Aren't missions something that only fully grown-up men and women should be considering?

Perhaps you have thought about missions but your thought is down the road, when you finish college or have your own family. Why should I even care about this?

A common issue when we think about missions is its place in church life. Many people wrongly consider that missions are the main goal of the Christian life. They may tend to think that the only Christians who are really serving God are the ones leaving everything behind to go abroad into the mission field. On the other hand, many believers set missions aside as something secondary in church life. So, which is it? Are missions the main goal of the church, or one among many?

Well, in fact, missions are a means to a greater goal. Let's illustrate this. Consider sports. Football, for example. Why do players run laps, pump iron, do push-ups, practice throwing, punting, or receiving? Why so many drills? Why all those hours spent perfecting movements and formations? The drills are not the goal. All of that is done to be better prepared for the main goal of scoring.

Think about the game itself. Is gaining yards the ultimate goal of football? No. The goal is to get the ball to the end zone. You may very well gain hundreds of yards during a match and yet repeatedly fail to score. The goal is to score. And the athletes practice a lot to be able to achieve this in several ways. Mission work is one way we get to the endzone. What is there at the end? The glory of God.

John Piper famously wrote that 'Missions is not the ultimate goal of the church. Worship is. Missions exist because worship doesn't.' Piper is making the point that even though missions have the immensely beneficial result of saving people from eternal punishment, ultimately, this is not the greater goal. God's glory is: His name being glorified in the salvation of sinners. And every single Christian, from the little children all the way to the elderly, should have God's glory in mind.

So, when we talk about missions, in reality we are talking about a way to make God's glory known more broadly, His name worshiped more intensely, His love received more deeply, His image in men restored in more places.

Consider, for example, Psalm 96. Notice the universal aspect of worship. Take note of the many mentions of the nations, the whole earth, etc.:

Oh sing to the Lord a new song;
*   sing to the Lord, all the earth!*
Sing to the Lord, bless his name;
*   tell of his salvation from day to day.*
Declare his glory among the nations,
*   his marvelous works among all the*
peoples!
For great is the Lord, and greatly to be
praised;
*   he is to be feared above all gods.*
For all the gods of the peoples are worthless
idols,
*   but the Lord made the heavens.*
Splendor and majesty are before him;
*   strength and beauty are in his sanctuary.*
Ascribe to the Lord, O families of the
peoples,
*   ascribe to the Lord glory and strength!*
Ascribe to the Lord the glory due his name;
*   bring an offering, and come into his*
courts!
Worship the Lord in the splendor of holiness;
*   tremble before him, all the earth!*
Say among the nations, 'The Lord reigns!
*   Yes, the world is established; it shall never*
be moved;
*   he will judge the peoples with equity.'*

*Let the heavens be glad, and let the earth
rejoice;*
    let the sea roar, and all that fills it;
    let the field exult, and everything in it!
*Then shall all the trees of the forest sing for
joy*
    before the Lord, for he comes,
    for he comes to judge the earth.
He will judge the world in righteousness,
    and the peoples in his faithfulness.

Do you see it? This is a Psalm talking about the name of Yahweh, the covenant God of Israel, being celebrated throughout the earth. His name is not to be praised only in the Promised Land. No. The psalmist's heart desire is for God's name to be feared and loved by families everywhere on the globe. He yearns for the nations to abandon their false gods. He longs to see the name of the one true God being worshiped everywhere.

How will this happen? Through missions. Piper again: 'Therefore, worship is the goal and the fuel of missions: Missions exists because worship doesn't. Missions is our way of saying: the joy of knowing Christ is not a private, or tribal, or national or ethnic privilege. It is for all. And that's why we go. Because we have tasted the joy of worshiping Jesus, and we want all the families of the earth included.'

We are living in a stage of human history in which people from every tongue, nation and tribe are being called to believe in Christ. This is only a temporary stage, however. When Christ returns, the age of missions will end. Worship, however, will remain forever.

So, to make a long story short: you should care about missions, because you should care about God's name being spread as far as the sun shines. You should care because you want to see people praising Christ from the Himalayan mountains to the remote islands of the Pacific, from the suburbs of California to the neighborhoods of Chicago. From the small villages of the Peruvian mountains to the river communities of the Ganges. From the tiny islands in the north of Scotland to the tiny islands in Oceania.

We are very quick to promote the name of those we love. We spend many hours online or in personal conversations defending the fame of the artists, athletes, or other people that we consider to be great. Thinking about missions is a way to do the same about someone who cares for you in a way that no one else ever will: the Savior who lived and died for you. Thinking about missions is not only for the missionaries or the boards who send them. It should be something close to the heart of every Christian because we have God's glory in mind. Are you beginning to see why mission is important?

Main Point

Missions are important ultimately because they are about God's glory.

Questions for Reflection

- What activities take up most of your time?
- In which ways are you glorifying God in your daily schedule?

2. Why Has God Decided to Reach the World in this Way?

Isn't reaching the nations through missions a bit overcomplicated? Why do it in such a way? Was that the only possible way? No. God could have given this mission to the angels. I am pretty sure that Gabriel and the others would love to go around the world spreading the good news. They would not be shy about it as we often are—they wouldn't care about feeling awkward as many of us do. God could commission the birds to fly around the world and sing the gospel story. God could have arranged the cloud formations to spell out the message of the cross in several languages. But no. He decided that the world would hear about Christ through those who already have come to Christ.

God's plan of salvation is wonderful indeed. From eternity, God decided to save a people for Himself through the work of Jesus Christ.

God the Son would become man and dwell among us. He would live about thirty-three years in perfect obedience to God's law. Every word, every thought and each of His actions would be sinless. He would then, as a perfect sacrifice, be offered up on the cross to pay for the eternal debt we owed God. On the third day, He would come back from the dead, raised up in glory by the power of the Holy Spirit. After a while He would ascend to heaven, from where He will come again to judge the living and the dead and complete the work of renovating heaven and earth. In the meantime, His people are being called to faith from every tribe, nation, and tongue. His Holy Spirit is giving life and sanctifying an enormous multitude of believers. What a glorious plan!

This is clear enough. Good news of salvation. The question is, how do people get to benefit from it? If a store in town has a huge sale, but you never get to hear about it, you can't go and benefit from the amazing discounts. Likewise, with the gospel, people actually need to believe in Christ to receive the blessings of Christ's work. And how do they come to believe? Paul explains in Romans 10:13-16 that:

For 'everyone who calls on the name of the Lord will be saved.' How then will they call on him in whom they have not believed? And how are they to believe in him of whom they have never heard? And how are they to hear without someone preaching? And how are they to preach unless they are sent? As it is written, 'How beautiful are the feet of those who preach the good news!'

What Paul is saying is that, for people to benefit from all that Jesus achieved on His mission, there must be other people going forth around the world in order to tell about Jesus. There is no way for the lost to believe in something they know nothing about. There is no way for people to believe in Jesus unless they hear about Him. Think about this: God chose to reach the nations through His own people preaching, evangelizing, and witnessing about Christ. The redeemed ones call others to join them. The adopted children go around the great orphanage that is this world and invite others to become family.

During His years of ministry when He was physically on earth, Jesus taught His disciples about the way of salvation and then sent them forth into the world as apostles, people who were sent in His name and authority to proclaim good news to the nations. The apostles had a very firm understanding that they were sent forth. The great missionary, Paul, explains his calling in this way:

> *But rise and stand upon your feet, for I have appeared to you for this purpose, to appoint you as a servant and witness to the things in which you have seen me and to those in which I will appear to you, delivering you from your people and from the Gentiles—to whom I am sending you to open their eyes, so that they may turn from darkness to light and from the power of Satan to God, that they may receive forgiveness of sins and a place among those who are sanctified by faith in me (Acts 26:16-18).*

Paul is seriously aware that he was saved by Christ and that he has a mission, which is to point people to Christ. The way for Gentiles to leave darkness and slavery and be saved would be through the ministry of the Word. This is the way unto salvation. This is how sins can be forgiven and a life of sanctification can begin, by the hearing of the preaching of God's Word. Would it not be horribly selfish of Paul to have been saved by this amazing grace and yet fail to proclaim such news to the Gentiles who lived in darkness?

We are not the apostle Paul, of course. And yet we, as believers, do have responsibility to tell forth the same good story of the blood-stained cross and the empty tomb. This is how people hear the gospel. This is how they can be saved. His is the glory in this way. That's how He designed it to be. Do you see that it is a great privilege to have this mission entrusted to us? As a believer, think of what a great privilege this is for you from your loving Father.

Main Point

God decided to reach the world through the preaching and witnessing of His own people.

Questions for Reflection

- Why is it that we often do not treat gospel proclamation as a privilege?
- What other biblical passages speak of God's glory being known by the nations?

3. Missions in the Old Testament: From Creation to Egypt

Did you know that one of the most important aspects of learning anything is asking questions? Often, we can be afraid to ask questions because we don't want to look stupid—I know that's true for me. Well, to grasp the Bible's teaching on missions, we need to ask questions.

In this chapter and the next, we're dealing with a very important question. Get ready. Here is the question for you: *Did God always plan to include the nations in salvation in Jesus Christ, or was that something brought up later?*

For example, imagine a young couple of newlyweds living in Philistia, right next to Israel. They are simply a young couple trying to make ends meet. One day, the husband goes to an Israelite city to buy bread for his family and hears people talking about how God saved them from the rule of Pharaoh. If he asks to know more about it and gets truly interested, could he become a follower of the Lord? Well, yes! *Really? But I thought salvation was restricted to the Jews?* Wrong!

In this and the next chapter, we will look at how the Old Testament points to a plan made before the foundation of the world to include the nations in the plan of salvation. *Wait. Don't you mean NEW Testament?* No. The Old one. We will get to the New. But it is very important that you understand this: God's plan all along was to reach the nations. This wasn't something that started in the New Testament. Let's begin in Genesis.

On the dark day when Adam and Eve committed treason by sinning against God and eating the fruit, a wonderful promise was made. It's in Genesis 3.15. God said that the serpent, though it appeared to have triumphed, would be defeated with a crushed head.

Until that moment, it seemed that all was lost. Humanity had failed in the simple task given by God and everything indicated that the hour of death was quickly approaching. God, however, had other plans. He promised that there would be a history of enmity between those who, like the serpent, are rebellious against God, and the one who, coming from the woman, would triumph over Satan. A simple promise of salvation that was made to the first couple. A promise that there would be a beautiful and powerful way out of the sin problem. Humanity would have a means of salvation.

Do notice this: Salvation to mankind. At this point in history, there was no Israel. There was only one couple, the forefathers of all nations.

As the history of the world progressed, God revealed more and more about this plan. He would save people from all over the world, not just from a small nation. At the time of Noah (Genesis 6-11), the world was restarted in the flood and God preserved a family from whom came the countless nations of the world. At that time in history, Israel didn't even exist. But many were being saved by faith in God's promises of salvation.

One fine day, God called a man from the land of Ur of the Chaldeans to be a blessing. God promised that countless people would be blessed in him and that he would have descendants as numerous as the stars in the sky or the sand in the sea. Abram was not raised in a believing household. He was a Chaldean who was reached by the grace of God and believed (you can read about it in Genesis 12 through 15). And how is this wonderful promise to reach the nations fulfilled?

First, let us remember that from Abram's physical descendants come the people of Israel. Through his son Isaac, and specifically through his grandson Jacob, the tribes of Israel arise. God sovereignly saved people through that blood line. Jacob himself, after a long career as a deceiver, was transformed by God and given the name 'Israel'. His sons gave rise to the tribes of what later came to be called the people of Israel. But that wasn't quick. Those men had to emigrate to Egypt because of a terrible famine in the Promised Land. And in about 400 years, those few men had become a huge crowd. People who suffered for being the Lord's people. They received from God a deliverer in Moses. God mightily rescued them from Pharaoh's bondage and set them on the path to Canaan. (The book of Exodus tells this story.)

So, yes, from Abraham's physical offspring came a great nation of worshipers of the true God. But don't forget something wonderful that the New Testament teaches us about this. The apostle Paul explains that the promise made to Abraham involved not only his physical descendants, but mainly his spiritual descendants. As he writes to the Gentiles of Galatia: 'And if you are Christ's, then you are Abraham's offspring, heirs according to promise' (Gal. 3:29).

In fact, many of Abraham's physical descendants actually rejected the Savior Jesus. In chapters 23 and 24 of Matthew, we read Jesus' words of the fearful punishments awaiting Jerusalem and the religious leaders who deceived people and rejected God's truth. They would be crushed in many ways. The nations, on the other hand, would believe.

This has always been the plan. There have always been among Abraham's descendants those who believed and who were, in fact, the Lord's people, but there were always also many who did not believe, who, in the end, were of the evil one. And the flip side of that is also true. Throughout Israel's history, people from other nations have joined the chosen people.

In Exodus itself, we are told that people from other nations took advantage of the mass departure from Egypt and left with the Israelites (Exod. 12:38). And it goes far beyond that. Consider, for example, Rahab of Jericho, who believed in the living God and was saved by her faith (see Josh. 6:22-25 and Heb. 11:31). Remember Ruth the Moabitess, who believed in the God of Israel and even entered the lineage of King David and of the Savior Jesus Christ (see the book of Ruth in the Bible).

Salvation, although for a period of history tied to Israel, was never exclusively Israel's. Indeed, they had a mission to function as a beacon, drawing the nations to the true Light. But that's a topic for the next chapter.

Main Point

God's eternal plan is to save a people for Himself from all tribes, tongues and nations.

Questions for Reflection

- Why do we tend to think of the gospel as something that belongs to a specific nation?
- Are there ways in which we are guilty of thinking that a given nation 'deserves' the gospel more than others?
- In which ways is God more glorified by saving such a diversity of people?

4. Old Testament: From Egypt to the Exile

There are many things about Christianity that make it a struggle for people to believe. While this is an obvious statement, there are things that even Christians can struggle with. We see one of these struggles through missions: Why did God choose Israel? Why not some other nation? Why choose any nation?

It wasn't because Israel was a holier or better nation. It was so they could *be* a holy nation. Sometimes, we can think of ourselves as so special and great that we kind of imagine it to be an obvious thing for God to save us. 'Sure, of course we are saved; we are God´s special people.' But we can easily forget that what makes us special is His love towards us, not anything that we did ourselves. God chose Israel to be a holy nation. What does that mean? As a teenager, I often imagined that being holy meant being perfect. Something defined by abstaining from all sorts of things and achieving a level of holiness to make God really proud of us. But, as I grew older, I realized that I could never achieve such a level. What does holiness mean, then? 'Holy' means set apart for a special usage. God speaks this clearly in Exodus 19:4-6:

You yourselves have seen what I did to the Egyptians, and how I bore you on eagles' wings and brought you to myself. Now therefore, if you will indeed obey my voice and keep my covenant, you shall be my treasured possession among all peoples, for all the earth is mine; and you shall be to me a kingdom of priests and a holy nation.' These are the words that you shall speak to the people of Israel.

God saved them to turn them into something special. A nation of priests. A people who should mediate between God and the world. A people who would represent Him and be protected by Him. God's law, delivered by Moses, involved provision for any and all foreigners who wished to become God's people (for example, Deut. 23:15-16; Exod. 12:48). There was no barrier! Everyone who believed would be saved and counted as one of the Lord's people. There are many examples in the Bible. Not only Rahab and Ruth, but Caleb, the famous spy. He came from a clan descending from Edom (see Josh. 14:6).

Follow the story with me. After some time established in the Promised Land, the people of Israel chose a king, a man named Saul. He didn't do very well; he ended up displeasing God deeply, and lost his post to David, a man after God's own heart. David continued the establishment of the kingdom, settling the capital of Israel in Jerusalem. There was one important project, however, that was still overdue, humanly speaking, of course.

From the Garden of Eden, God had given man the responsibility to cultivate and guard the earth. Tend and care. Man was to develop that place in honor of God and for His glory, a place where truth, goodness and justice would dwell. After humanity failed to do so, God gave us previews of the day when He would solve the world's problem, restoring a holy place for His people to live in harmony with creation and the Creator. God gave us two important physical samples or previews of this.

First, the tabernacle, revealed to Moses to be built in the desert and to function as a sort of mobile temple (See Exod. 35-40). Later on, the tabernacle was replaced by the temple. Both tabernacle and temple had the same goal: to show symbolically that God was with His people in blessing and provision. Back to David: he knew that the temple had to be built, but God didn't let him fulfill that mission (2 Samuel 7). It fell to his son, Solomon. And, at the inauguration of this wonderful temple, the king prayed wonderfully, and here is part of what he said:

Likewise, when a foreigner, who is not of your people Israel, comes from a far country for your name's sake (for they shall hear of your great name and your mighty hand, and of your outstretched arm), when he comes and prays toward this house, hear in heaven your dwelling place and do according to all for which the foreigner calls to you, in order that all the peoples of the earth may know your name and fear you, as do your people Israel, and that they may know that this house that I have built is called by your name (1 Kings 8:41-43).

The king's prayer includes the request that people from other nations would hear about God and pray. Solomon's desire was that not only the people of Israel, but the whole planet would fear the Lord. One famous example of this happening is when the Queen of the distant kingdom of Sheba hears about Solomon and the name of the Lord and travels to Jerusalem to hear more (1 Kings 10). A house of prayer for all peoples, as Jesus said (Matt. 21:13). A place where little by little people from all nations could come and hear about the true God, by faith sacrifice to the true God and if they wanted to, become part of God's people.

However, this was not meant to be the only way in which the nations would know about the Lord. The book of Jonah is a beautiful example of this principle, with the prophet being sent to carry a message of repentance to the mighty and wicked city of Nineveh. And many believed! In the Old Testament we do see instances of God's people going out of Canaan to make the name of the Lord known and feared.

Consider how God wonderfully was able to transform even the result of His people's unfaithfulness into missionary blessing. Think about the Babylonian exile: because of the unfaithfulness of the tribe of Judah, the Lord brought judgment upon them through the wicked Babylonians. Many were taken captive to Babylon. The book of Daniel tells us how a few young men remained faithful to God and served Him even in exile. And, more than that, they served as faithful witnesses of the true God.

Something similar happened later on. Babylon fell and the Persian empire took its place. In the biblical book of Esther, we can read the story of how Jews living in that land tried to live and survive a genocidal attempt by Haman, a wicked man who descended from Israel's old enemies, the Amalekites. A lot happens in the story, and we cannot go into detail here: suffice to say that God works in mysterious ways and instead of His people being murdered they are saved and, at the end of the story many people from several nations join God's people (Esther 8.17).

We could turn to many other examples in the Old Testament, but I trust that the point has been made. Salvation was never exclusive to the people of Israel. It was through such a nation that the other nations would come to hear about God. And in the New Testament, it becomes clear how this would take place.

The Psalms are full of calls for the nations to worship the true God. Let us look at one example. Psalm 67 says:

May God be gracious to us and bless us
  and make his face to shine upon us, Selah
that your way may be known on earth,
  your saving power among all nations.
Let the peoples praise you, O God;
  let all the peoples praise you!
Let the nations be glad and sing for joy,
  for you judge the peoples with equity
  and guide the nations upon earth. Selah
Let the peoples praise you, O God;
  let all the peoples praise you!
The earth has yielded its increase;
  God, our God, shall bless us.
God shall bless us;
  let all the ends of the earth fear him!

Notice that the psalmist asks God to bless His people, in the expectation that this would serve to attract people from other nations to love Him.

Do you see it? The psalmist uses words from Aaron's blessing (Num. 6:22-27) on Israel. And he explains that this blessing ultimately serves for the people of the earth to worship the Lord. In fact, there are many psalms that point to people all over the world being called to worship the true God. God's plan was never to restrict salvation to one people. The salvation promised to Adam will reach the entire earth. And the New Testament shows how this happens. We'll see it in the next chapter.

Main Point

In the Old Testament, God sets forth His plan to make His name feared and loved by the nations.

Questions for Reflection

- Why is it that we tend to think of holiness as some sort of perfection through which God may love us? Can we ever achieve such holiness by ourselves?
- How does God deal with His global church in order to make His name known?
- How would you explain to another Christian about the way of salvation in the Old Testament? Do you clearly understand that it was by grace through faith in the promised Messiah?

5. Missions in the New Testament

A man called B.B. Warfield once said that the Old Testament is like a dark room filled with furniture. It has couches, chairs, a table, etc. all over the room, but there's no light. The New Testament is the light that shines in that room. Other than the light, nothing has changed about the room. The furniture is all there and in the same place, but now you can see it more clearly. In other words, the Old & New Testaments are unified and work together. Now let's see how the New Testament helps us see the Old more clearly.

Just like the previous two chapters, many books could be written about this topic. The New Testament itself could even be described as a book that details the missionary work of Jesus (coming from heaven into Earth) and then the missionary work of His disciples (going to the nations). The New Testament speaks a lot to the issue of missions, and, of course, we will only have the time to briefly reflect on some of what it teaches.

When you look at the genealogy of Jesus (His family tree), you should not miss the fact that several Gentiles are included. Yes, Jesus was a Jew. And yet many of His forefathers were not.

Look at Matthew 1, for example. There is mention of Gentiles, such as Rahab and Ruth. If you examine the genealogy in Luke 3, however, you will see even more, for you will see several men who come before Abraham, and who could in no way be considered Jews. By the way, while many Jews rejected Jesus, in His time on earth, He had some very interesting dealings with Gentiles, such as the centurion (Matt. 8:5-13) and the Samaritan woman (John 4).

Jesus came into this world with a mission. In short: He would live a perfectly sinless life, He would die on a cross for the sins of His people, He would rise from the dead on the third day. He had a lot to do in terms of His three offices of prophet, priest, and king. During His time on earth, He primarily sought the people of Israel, who, by and large, rejected Him. But His plan was not to be foiled. At the end of the gospels, we have the Great Commission. The one in Matthew is usually the most used to understand what Jesus requires of the disciples. This is how it goes:

Now the eleven disciples went to Galilee, to the mountain to which Jesus had directed them. And when they saw him they worshiped him, but some doubted. And Jesus came and said to them, 'All authority in heaven and on earth has been given to me. Go therefore and make disciples of all nations, baptizing them in the name of the Father and of the Son and of the Holy Spirit, teaching them to observe all that I have commanded you. And behold, I am with you always, to the end of the age (Matt. 28:16-20).

Basically, Jesus tells them to reach the nations with the gospel message. Notice, however, that this is not in some detached way, perhaps going from town to town and shouting something about repentance before hastily moving to the next village.

Perhaps you've seen a movie where someone carries around a sign that reads 'The End is Near!' and they're screaming at people to repent and believe. Now, I'm not questioning everyone who's ever done that—maybe they had a heart of sincerity. I may question the movie, because the portrayal isn't always positive. That said, the Great Commission in Matthew gave a strong relational component to spreading the gospel.

Jesus commands them to make disciples. This means adding people to the believing community (the church) through the sacrament of baptism. And this means teaching them how to live as Christians. The Great Commission requires Jesus' disciples to intentionally leave their area and seek people from the nations, from all the different ethnic groups and teach them the gospel in its entirety. Just as Christ lived in this world, so we, as His disciples, are called to live among others and walk with them to make disciples.

When we come to the book of Acts, we see how this happens. In Acts 1:8, Jesus tells the disciples that: 'But you will receive power when the Holy Spirit has come upon you, and you will be my witnesses in Jerusalem and in all Judea and Samaria, and to the end of the earth.'

We could very well divide Acts into three large sections, showing how, as predicted, the gospel spreads in Jerusalem (chapters 1-7), then in Judea and Samaria (chapters 8-12) and, finally, to the ends of the world (chapters 13-28). This is the time in which we live. The gospel is going forth to all the nations. God is calling a people for Himself, a new holy nation made from both Jews and Gentiles who believe in Jesus. In the epistles, much is explained about God´s wonderful plan of making a new nation, a new country made from both Gentiles and Jews. (See, for example, Eph. 2:11-3:7).

The New Testament explains the mission in several ways. For example, Jesus tells us a very interesting story in Matthew 22: 1-12. The king is going to throw a wedding feast for his son. He invites his subjects, but they reject the invitation. In some cases, with indifference; in others, with violence. The king then decides that the invitation will be extended to all who wish to attend. His servants are ordered to go everywhere carrying invitations so that all kinds of people are invited to the party. Of course, Jesus was explaining that the Jews were refusing to take part in the feast of Jesus. And the nations were all invited: Bolivians, Americans, Britains, Brazilians, Dominicans,

Polish, people from every ethnic group under the sun.

We can think of evangelism and missions in these festive terms: What we do is deliver invitations. We are authorized, in fact, commissioned by the king to give them to whoever is nearby. To our family members, classmates, co-workers, neighbors, etc. We even deliver invitations to those who are far away. In the mountains of Nepal, in the forests of Congo, in the islands of the South Pacific, in the gigantic cities of Japan. In fact, we are all the fruit of the work of people who left their own land at some point in history to bring invitations to those who did not have them.

This is, by the way, the main function of missionaries: to deliver invitations to the wedding feast of Jesus and His people. Of course, the missionary can take care of other things in the meantime, but without losing focus. And yes, these invitations need to be translated into other languages and explained. That is why cross-cultural missions pose specific challenges. How do we witness the gospel to people with different languages, different cultural backgrounds, and different lifestyles from ours? We will deal with that next.

Main Point

In the New Testament, the complete plan of salvation unfolds and we begin to see the nations being reached for Christ.

Questions for Reflection

- Do you know how the gospel message came to your country and even more specifically, to your part of the country? It is well worth learning about how your ancestors came to believe!
- In which region of the world do we find more areas without the light of the gospel? Try to find out!
- How would you explain to another Christian about the way of salvation in the Old Testament? Do you clearly understand that it was by grace through faith in the promised Messiah?

6. What is a Transcultural Mission?

Transcultural missions? Have you ever heard such an expression? As I said earlier, it's always good to ask questions about a subject, so here's a new one for you.

We often speak of transcultural missions, but many have no idea of what that means. Or perhaps the mind goes to far-away islands, lost jungles, cannibal tribes, weird clothing, and even weirder food. Well, those things are indeed transcultural, but there is much more to consider. How does transcultural mission differ from regular mission work?

Everyone knows that sharing our faith is not a simple task. We are ashamed, afraid of being mocked, afraid of not knowing what to say, etc. Witnessing about the gospel is wonderful, but it does come with many difficulties.

When we think about the difficulty of preaching the gospel, we know that there are great barriers. What we sometimes overlook is that, when it comes to communicating the gospel to people of other cultures, there are even more difficulties. This is what we call transcultural missions. In other words, missions that involve overcoming cultural barriers.

Well, isn't it just going out and preaching? In a way, yes. But when we are concerned about effectively communicating the gospel, we need to take some difficulties into account.

Take Paul, for example. He took the gospel to many different regions. Although there was great cultural similarity in the cities where he preached because of Roman rule and Greek heritage, each location had its specific flavor.

What do I mean by 'specific flavor'? Think about it this way. Do you dress the same way as someone from a foreign country? In some ways, maybe, but in many ways, no. Each country has a 'flavor' if you will. Or think about all differences in terms of music, food, rituals, holidays, sports ... every culture has its own distinct features!

When Paul preached in a synagogue with Jews who knew the Old Testament, he sought to show through his preaching that Jesus was the promised Messiah. When he preached in a public context where people had no idea what the Old Testament was, he took a different approach, as exemplified in his sermon on Mars Hill in Athens (Acts 17). It's not that he left the Bible aside, but rather that he taught the worldview and the content of Scripture in a different way.

Think about how many barriers there are.

To begin with, there are linguistic barriers. In many parts of the world when the missionary arrives, there is no Bible in the language of that people, and in most situations, many of the local people do not speak another language. Thus, there is a long process of trying to learn and translate the Scripture into that language, while relationships are established, and the message is communicated. Learning a foreign language to the point of being able to communicate well, and teaching concepts like sin and grace can take a long time. So, not only do we dress differently to people of a foreign country, but we also talk differently. Not just various languages, but even slang terms.

And then there are still other cultural barriers. A missionary needs to learn a lot about how to enter a community. How do people treat each other on a daily basis? How do they eat? How do you greet each other? What are the basic rules of etiquette? How do women and children behave? What are the customs regarding weddings, funerals, celebrations? A lack of knowledge of all of these can complicate the missionary's familiarity with the people and make it difficult to communicate the gospel. Or worse, it may be that the missionary unwittingly causes tremendous offense and turns his or her audience against him.

To think about language a bit more, the challenge of adapting language to culture is a major barrier. I know that in many cases there are exaggerated analogies that end up distorting the message, however we must remember that there must always be some level of *contextualization*. But what is this?

Contextualizing means making the message understandable to the listener. For example, when we warn a three-year-old child not to touch an electrical outlet, we don't say: 'If you touch it, an electrical current can occur that will cause cardiorespiratory arrest that can lead to death and cause serious burns.' All of this is true, but it is beyond the understanding of the small child. But we say, 'It will hurt a lot!' Or words to that effect.

We want them to understand the warning above all. The older the child, the more explanation will be given. This is contextualizing. We all experience it. When we are going to tell a story of what happened on a trip to the beach, we include more or less details depending on who we are telling, whether the listener is familiar with the location, the characters, the events or not. If needed, we include explanations about who the people are, about what the weather was like. We adapt the speech to make it understandable. We provide information, and we seek to explain things in a way that the listener can grasp.

And that's biblical. Paul, in his letters, often uses sporting or military metaphors to make the complex spiritual and theological issues he is explaining understandable. The Bible itself is God's Word put to us in human terms.

Whenever we talk about the gospel, we need to help people where they are to understand such deep truths. In a transcultural context, this is even more difficult. I hope you realize how challenging transcultural missions can be. And I didn't even get into issues such as homesickness, health difficulties, finances and much more.

Transcultural missions are difficult but necessary. They are part of fulfilling the Great Commission. Do you realize that we must send well qualified people to this task? In my view, transcultural missionaries need to be even better prepared than local pastors. They should, in addition to all theological and ministerial training, receive specific training for the issues they will have to face in the cross-cultural toil.

What does this have to do with you? Maybe think about cross-cultural missions in your context. Perhaps you have someone in your school or community who isn't from your immediate context. Maybe they are from a different city, state, or country. Maybe they belong to a different ethnic group. Maybe they even believe in a different religion. You see, you have a different culture to deal with and you can begin praying about ways in which you could contextualize the gospel in a way they can understand. But this takes a great amount of time.

I hope this brings you to a greater appreciation of what is involved in transcultural missions. We need people who are well prepared to think biblically through many issues. People who are willing to leave their cultural comfort zone and serve others through gospel proclamation. Let us ask the Lord of the harvest to send even more workers!

Main Point

It is not easy to preach the gospel to people of different cultures. There is some extra effort required in finding ways to make the message connect with those who hear.

Questions for Reflection

- Have you ever had experience of trying to communicate with someone with a very different cultural background from you?
- How can we better prepare to reach people very different from us?
- What do you think the major difficulties are for you when you want to communicate with people who are very different from you?

7. Missions in a Relativistic World

In our current cultural climate, at least in the Western World, there is an issue we need to address. Considering that we bring the gospel to people with wildly different backgrounds, stories, beliefs and practices, the question arises often: *Isn't it wrong, or at least rude, to try and impose our beliefs upon other people?*

Well, of course we do not want to be rude about it. And yes, much evil has been done under the banner of supposedly taking forth the gospel to the nations. And yet, the most loving thing we can do to a dying world is precisely to obey God´s command to preach the gospel. We are, after all, called to give the reasons of our faith with gentleness and respect (1 Pet. 3:15,16). And yet, we do have the mandate to tell people about the gospel. The very idea that there are universal truths has been under fire in the western world.

Let's consider it in this way. If the gospel is true, and indeed the only way of salvation is through faith in Christ, why would it be wrong or rude to tell people? Would you rather drown or have someone rescue you from the ocean waves, even if being rescued hurts your pride somewhat?

But if the gospel is really just a message that makes us feel better about life, or perhaps a man-made system of controlling people then yes, let's leave people alone and not bother them with it. However, if the gospel is indeed the last and only hope of all people groups spread around the globe, then, by all means, we must tell them. That is our mission. And that is the loving attitude. We are not able to make them believe; we cannot open their heart and implant faith into it. But we can love God in obeying His call, and love people by telling them about the good news of salvation in Christ. Thankfully, sometime in the past, people believed the gospel seriously enough to take it across the Atlantic. Had they not done so, we here in the Americas would not know this news and would not be saved.

My country, Brazil, received missionaries from several denominations. My own denomination, Presbyterianism, was first started in Brazil when a man named Ashbel Green Simonton, after hearing a sermon preached by Charles Hodge at Princeton Seminary, decided to go into mission work and chose Brazil as his field. I am glad that he did. All of us have someone else to thank for receiving the Good News of salvation.

Paul explains to us something very important about every human being. In Romans 1:18-25, he writes that man knows something about God's existence merely by living in God's world. However, being the guilty, sinful people that we are, we strive to suppress the truth in unrighteousness. What does that mean? That nobody examines the world and the evidence for God's existence in a neutral or objective way. We are by our sinful natures biased toward claiming that there is no God.

So, this is the natural situation of mankind. Man, everywhere and in all ages, seeks to avoid the truth about God and about himself. The time in which we live is no different; people actively seek to suppress God's truth. The most common manner to do this nowadays is by claiming that there is no such thing as objective truth, that all truth is personal and particular, and that we should never act as if we have a better view on reality than others do.

We should not fear this. In the end, mankind is always trying to find one way or another to escape from the truth. What we must do is bring forth the truth in love. The whole gospel, the message that God provides in Jesus Christ, is the only way to avoid His holy wrath. The way is open for salvation. All men have the same need everywhere. People from the Middle Ages may be very different from us and from our parents. And surely people who come along in the next century will be very different from us. But all people have the same need: Jesus Christ. Our duty is to proclaim Him. It is not harder for the Holy Spirit to open up the heart of an unbeliever in our days than it was in the days of the apostles.

Of course, by this I do not mean that we should be blunt or obnoxious about it. By understanding the spirit of our age, we can be winsome and clever in finding bridges to communicate the gospel to our peers, making the message clear to our age. This is, however, a topic for another day. For now, keep this in mind: telling someone the gospel is the most loving thing you can do for them.

Main Point

The gospel is mankind's greatest need, no matter the time and age in which we live.

Questions for Reflection

- Do you tend to think of religious convictions as something to be kept private? If yes, why do you think that is the case?
- How can we answer someone who says that all religions are basically the same?
- How do we love people in this day and age with regards to the gospel?

8. How Have Globalization and the Digital Revolution Changed Things?

In this chapter, we will briefly consider some of the changes in the world in recent years that have shaped the way in which we go about our Great Commission. God is guiding the world in His providence, and wisely has led mankind through all sorts of technological change.

DIGITAL REVOLUTION

I grew up without a smartphone. Actually, it was only after finishing my doctorate that I finally purchased one, around 2012. I know that by then, smartphones had been around for a while, and yet they were not everywhere as they are nowadays. Most people in our cities, in most countries, have some sort of electronic device capable of accessing the internet. People use all sorts of ways to communicate online. Play, work, entertainment, religion, relationships....
All of these have been reshaped by the digital

revolution. How does that change missions? Well, there are a lot of positive results from it.

Connectivity does play an important role in maintaining relationship and encouragement. Many times, life is lonely for missionaries. By being able to keep in touch more frequently, they can be more actively encouraged, strengthened, and heard. Social media can help in the publicity of the missionary work. Today, it is much easier to follow the work of the missionaries abroad, raise awareness of the issues and challenges they face and even hold them to a higher level of accountability.

Teaching and training can take on new formats with the increasing connectivity around the world. Many missionaries far away on the field can be taught all sorts of ministerial and non-ministerial skills while on the mission field.

GLOBALIZATION

It is crazy to think about the challenges faced by early missionaries. This doesn't mean that missions today or in the future won't have challenges, but let's think a bit about early missions.

For example, it took John Paton many months of rough sea travel to get to the New Hebrides and do his mission work in the 1800s.

Throughout history, missionaries in foreign fields often took the better part of a year to even get to the field, let alone begin the work itself. They often lived in severe isolation. They had to wait many days and weeks to send and receive letters, to get supplies or any kind of help.

Nowadays, if we have the money, we can be pretty much anywhere in the world within ninety-six hours. You can wake up in New York, have lunch in Los Angeles at LAX and wake up in Tokyo the next morning. Of course, there are still islands and communities within forests that are not easy to reach. But the development of air travel has reduced the cost, both in terms of time and of money, to get to distant places.

Today, all this is much simpler. Sending missionaries, sending supplies, making field visits, getting missionaries back for a break, sending teams out for short-term relief, and much more is made easier in our days. Of course, there are still many situations that cause difficulties. Pandemics, wars, natural disasters, and other barriers follow and will continue to limit the movement of missionaries. But today, we find it much easier to send out teams and support them in the mission field.

A few years ago, I had the privilege of spending a week in Kathmandu, the capital of Nepal, helping with the training of church planters. It's not an easy journey, of course. But I left my city, Brasília, and with stops in São Paulo and Doha, I was face to face and talking about the Christian faith with brothers in Nepal in less than forty-eight hours. In ten days, I was back home. That would have been impossible a few decades ago.

Of course, with the advancement of technology and its availability, the same course could easily have been given online, without me leaving my city. Obviously, a lot would be lost, but that's not the point here. The important thing is to realize that we live in a time when technological advances, freedom of travel, and many other realities transform our missionary task and offer many possibilities. Being aware of what God is doing in the world helps us tremendously to find ways to be wiser in fulfilling our commission.

You see, all of this makes our task a lot easier. Which means that more is being put into our hands and we must act responsibly with these divine gifts. Ease of traveling around the world should take us beyond mere tourism and help us think more strategically about missionary possibilities. The vast worldwide network of connectivity tremendously broadens our horizons of study, work, and play, but it should also show us ways to serve God better through reaching out to the nations. May we know how to use the gifts and talents that God puts in our hands for His glory!

Main Point

Any age in which we live has its own challenges and advantages to mission work.

Questions for Reflection

- Can you think of three ways in which transportation technology has made mission work easier?
- Are there, however, disadvantages that we face today with all the technology we have?
- In which ways is the church failing to utilize advantages that our age gives us for the proclamation of the gospel?

9. The End of Missions

I don't know about you, but there are many things I look forward to when I leave this earth. And many of them have to do with certain things ending. When I die and am with Jesus, my sin will come to an end. All sickness will end. Sadness and injustice will end. Anxiety and depression will cease. It's funny, however, that some good things will end as well.

Our mission shall end. Yes, we live in the age of missions. Since Jesus' ascent and before He returns to make all things new and judge the world, we are in the timespan of calling the nations to repentance and faith in Christ.

We will not have this mission forever! We are at the stage of carrying the baton, as in a relay race. Many have already carried the mission by taking the gospel and making disciples of every tribe, language and nation. Now, it's up to us. One day we will end our career and others will continue the mission. But this will not be endless: it's just for a while. Until our Lord Jesus returns in power and glory to judge the world and inaugurate the New Heavens and a New Earth.

At the beginning of the book, we argued that missions are not an end in themselves, but an instrument for the greater end of glorifying God. When Christ returns, those who have believed in Him throughout all ages will be able to delight in Him perpetually in worship, fellowship, and service in the world made whole, in the earth free from sin and its horrible results. Today is the time to face the darkness and bring the light of the gospel. But that will no longer be necessary when the whole world is illuminated by the glory of the Lamb. All that remains for us then will be to celebrate eternally the triumph of the one who is for us.

The Bible tells us that the Lord Jesus, when dealing with His most difficult mission, kept in mind the joy of what would be the result of His effort:

Therefore, since we are surrounded by so great a cloud of witnesses, let us also lay aside every weight, and sin which clings so closely, and let us run with endurance the race that is set before us, looking to Jesus, the founder and perfecter of our faith, who for the joy that was set before him endured the cross, despising the shame, and is seated at the right hand of the throne of God. (Heb. 12:1, 2)

It makes all the difference in the world to know that the mission will be successful and that the joy of triumph will come. With us, it is no different. Like the mother who endures the birth pangs for the hope of the joy of having a baby, or the athlete who endures the muscle pain and exhaustion of training with the hope of the joy of the trophy, the Lord's people advance in their mission with hope. It's not easy.

There are many opponents who seek to hinder the task of making disciples. There are many who try to stop us from pushing forward. Many of us have been killed for trying to carry on these wonderful truths of Christ's work. But we have before us the joy of knowing that one day we will be in triumph with Christ. Together with us will be those who were called and believed. And one day, the glory of the Lord Jesus will be recognized and loved in every part of the world. Good news, isn't it?

Main Point

One day, our mission will end, and the saved will be free to glorify God and enjoy Him through eternity.

Questions for Reflection

- How does the knowledge that our mission will come to a successful end encourage us now?
- Does it make you happy to imagine that you will spend eternity with God's people from all tongues, nations, and tribes?
- What do you long for the most about eternity?

Appendix A: What Now?

'Well, missions then. I am sold on the idea', you may say. Or at least I pray that you do. 'And I will begin paying more attention to my church's mission festival and even consider donating some money.' Good! But the matter is much deeper. *You* are a missionary. If you follow Jesus, if you are a disciple, then yes, the Great Commission is yours as well. You may not be called to go into full-time ministry, let alone transcultural missions. But you have, nevertheless, responsibility.

Dr. Elias Medeiros often speaks about 'not wasting our geography'. Consider this. In your own neighborhood, apartment complex, office building, gym, basketball team, online gaming community, there are many unbelievers. Which is simpler? Sending missionaries to these groups, or using the believers who are already there?

Let me point you to a very interesting conversion story in the gospels. In Mark 2:13-17, the Bible tells us that Jesus called a man named Matthew (also known as Levi) to follow Him. Matthew was a tax collector: someone who worked for the Roman Empire, and who therefore was not in good favor with other Jews. Matthew follows Jesus. And more than that, he immediately looks for an opportunity to take others to meet Jesus as well. Who are those people? The ones who used to work with him. He realizes that few people would be better placed to take those other tax collectors to Jesus than one of them. Of course, the message could reach them in a variety of ways. But why not through someone who was already one of them, knew their way of life, customs, language and sins? Likewise, you are also part of groups that need to hear about Christ. And who do you think is closest, perhaps even more apt to carry that message? Yes, you.

Prayer is involved. Of course, we may take this aspect for granted. After all, we know that we can do nothing apart from Christ (John 15:5). I love that, at the end of Ephesians, Paul asks the people to pray for him, so that 'words may be given to me in opening my mouth boldly to proclaim the mystery of the gospel.' (Eph 6:19). Here is the great preacher, theologian, apostle and missionary Paul, asking for help! Specifically help in prayer, so that when he has occasion to preach, he may have the words and the boldness for such a task. Paul knows that he is not sufficient. We should never forget this. Christ is with us every day until the end.

Here are some useful actions for you to better develop your comprehension about missions:

- Read missionary biographies! I have found that missionary biographies can be quite interesting and stirring of the heart. And they help a lot in preventing romantic ideas about the mission field. John Piper has a very fine book series called *The Swans Are Not Silent* that has short biographies of many relevant people in church history, including many missionaries. They are available online for free at desiringgod.org. You may want to read about John Paton, Hudson Taylor, Adoniram Judson, David Brainerd, among others...

- Missions committee: Your church likely has some sort of missions committee. It is very possible that your local church supports some missionaries. Get to know them! Correspond with them. Pray for them and stay updated with their lives. Missionaries love when folks back home show them love and support.

- Consider a short-term mission trip! This may be very useful to help you understand better what mission work is all about.

- Get involved in outreach activities of your church, or perhaps bible study groups at your school. This will help you!

May the Lord bless you and encourage you!

Appendix B: Other Books on this Topic

There are many good resources for those who wish to dive deeper. Here are a few good ones. Of course, no mere human book is perfect. You should always compare them to the Bible.

Bavinck. J.H. *An Introduction to the Science of Mission* (Presbyterian & Reformed Publishing, 1993).

DeYoung, Kevin. *What is the Mission of the Church? Making Sense of Social Justice, Shalom, and the Great Commission* (Crossway, 2011).

Kaiser, Walter C, Jr. *Mission in the Old Testament: Israel as a Light to the Nations* (Grand Rapids: Baker, 2012).

Neill, Stephen. *A History of Christian Missions* (Penguin, 1964).

Piper, John. *Let the Nations be Glad. The Supremacy of God in Missions* (Baker Academic, 2010).

Piper, John. *21 Servants of Sovereign Joy: Faithful, Flawed, and Fruitful* (Crossway, 2018).

Schlehlein, Paul. *John G. Paton. Missionary to the Cannibals of the South Seas* (Banner of Truth, 2017).

Sills, David. *The Missionary Call: Find Your Place in God's Plan for the World* (Moody Publishers, 2018).

Tucker, Ruth. *From Jerusalem to Irian Jaya: A Biographical History of Christian Missions* (Zondervan, 2004).

Wright, Christopher J. H. *The Mission of God: Unlocking the Bible's Grand narrative* (IVP Academic, 2006).

Watch out for other forthcoming books in the
Track series, including:

Reformed Youth Ministries (RYM) exists to serve the Church in reaching and equipping youth for Christ. Passing on the faith to the next generation has been RYM's mission since it began. In 1972, three youth workers who shared a passion for biblical teaching to high school students surveyed the landscape of youth ministry conferences. What they found was a primary emphasis on fun and games, not God's Word. They launched a conference that focused on the preaching and teaching of God's Word – RYM. Over the last five decades RYM has grown from a single summer conference into three areas of ministry: conferences, training, and resources.

- **Conferences:** RYM hosts multiple summer conferences for local church groups in a variety of locations across the United States. Conferences are for either middle school or high school students and their leaders.
- **Training:** RYM launched an annual Youth Leader Training (YLT) event in 2008. YLT is

for anyone serving with youth in the local church. YLT has grown steadily through the years and is now offered in multiple locations. RYM also offers a Church Internship Program in partnering local churches, youth leader coaching and youth ministry consulting services.

- **Resources:** RYM offers a growing array of resources for leaders, parents, and students. Several BIble studies are available as free downloads (new titles regularly added). RYM hosts multiple podcasts available on numerous platforms: The Local Youth Worker, Parenting Today, and The RYM Student Podcast. To access free downloads, for podcast information, and access to many additional ministry tools visit us on the web – rym.org.

RYM is a 501(c)(3) non-profit organization. Our mission is made possible through the generous support of individuals, churches, foundations and businesses that share our mission to serve the Church in reaching and equipping youth for Christ. If you would like to partner with RYM in reaching and equipping the next generation for Christ please visit rym.org/donate.

Christian Focus Publications

Our mission statement —

STAYING FAITHFUL

In dependence upon God we seek to impact the world through literature faithful to His infallible Word, the Bible. Our aim is to ensure that the Lord Jesus Christ is presented as the only hope to obtain forgiveness of sin, live a useful life and look forward to heaven with Him.

Our books are published in four imprints:

CHRISTIAN
FOCUS

Popular works including biographies, commentaries, basic doctrine and Christian living.

CHRISTIAN
HERITAGE

Books representing some of the best material from the rich heritage of the church.

MENTOR

Books written at a level suitable for Bible College and seminary students, pastors, and other serious readers. The imprint includes commentaries, doctrinal studies, examination of current issues and church history.

CF4•K

Children's books for quality Bible teaching and for all age groups: Sunday school curriculum, puzzle and activity books; personal and family devotional titles, biographies and inspirational stories — because you are never too young to know Jesus!

Christian Focus Publications Ltd,
Geanies House, Fearn, Ross-shire,
IV20 1TW, Scotland, United Kingdom.
www.christianfocus.com
blog.christianfocus.com